Omena Bay

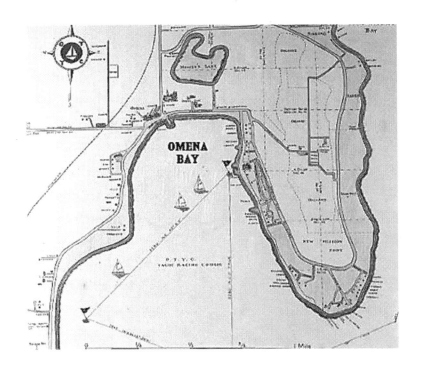

Gail Griffin

Winner of the Wilder Series Poetry Book Prize

Two Sylvias Press

Two Sylvias Press
PO Box 1524
Kingston, WA 98346
twosylviaspress@gmail.com

Cover Photo: "Still Waters on Omena Bay" by Bill Betts
Cover Design: Kelli Russell Agodon
Book Design: Annette Spaulding-Convy
Author Photo Credit: Fran Dwight Photography

Special Note from Photographer Bill Betts:

I dedicate this cover photo to the loving memory of Carole Taylor Betts, my wife and adventurous life partner of 54 years, who introduced me to, and shared with me, the infectious spirit of peace and tranquility that comes from the natural environment of Omena, Michigan.

Created with the belief that *great writing is good for the world,* Two Sylvias Press mixes modern technology, classic style, and literary intellect with an eco-friendly heart. We draw our inspiration from the poetic literary talent of Sylvia Plath and the editorial business sense of Sylvia Beach. We are an independent press dedicated to publishing the exceptional voices of writers.

For more information about Two Sylvias Press please visit:
www.twosylviaspress.com

First Edition. Created in the United States of America.

ISBN 978-1-948767-19-4

Praise for *Omena Bay Testament*

Gail Griffin finds inspiration from all the corners of life, from the bold headlines to the dark fairytales of childhood. In all of the conversations, lessons, and silences, Griffin finds new questions, moments to celebrate, and a pain that hardens us into something unburnable. These powerful poems hold to the body's latest troubles, the troubles we set down for the last time, and the "bright ferocity of what's left." Rich with revelations of the self and the world, this book offers us a testament of attention as we move into new seasons and new shores. **—Traci Brimhall**

৪০

Gail Griffin's "Omena Bay Testament" takes us across landscapes of winter and water through the possibility of love and the tragedy of death to a ravishing moment where there is nothing left to want. An accomplished nonfiction writer, Griffin captures the fullness and limitations of being with remarkable depth and tenacity in her debut collection of poetry and prose. *I'm cloaked in the invisibility that comes to women at a certain point,* she writes, and it is from that place of being off-stage where her narratives— harrowing, nuanced, layered—brilliantly forge a path between past and present, the living and the dead. I can't think of another book that gifts its readers with such a breadth of time and experience. Sweeping and seamless, Griffin shifts between wide and exacting gazes, from poems of quiet interiority to the larger breaking world, especially with her masterful sequence in response to news excerpts. This book is a life; it is a gift of integrity and lasting art. **—Jennifer K. Sweeney**

Table of Contents

In memory of my mother

Barbara Jeanne Hanna

1915 – 2004

who first told me I was a writer

"Creation, then, is the only axiom—"

~ Conrad Hilberry, "Wise Man"

I

This Edge

Omena Bay Testament

Truth be told, I've probably fucked my last.
It's something, bidding all that noise goodbye.
Fucked my last, screamed my last, galloped my last,
done my last back dive, taken my last star turn,
drowning in roses. Hit my last high C,
though I've got a low C in me, if that counts.
I'd say I had my fill but I've also lied my last.
I never had enough, not even close.

On this late afternoon Omena Bay is quiet,
mercurial silver under a low and broken sky.
Three sailboats bob at rest, two kayaks slide awry.
I have a beer, a book, nowhere to be.
I'm cloaked in the invisibility that comes
to women at a certain point. The bay
curves like a hand closing on something fragile.
I've driven past but never stopped before.

I have time on my hands, too much, too little,
depending. Mine is a body at rest remaining.
I've almost made my peace with the narrow
bed at my rental up the road. I've learned
to keep my arms in, not to roll around.
I'd prefer a queen, but then I'd also like
perfect pitch, a cooling planet, 20/20 vision,
and my final fuck still pending.

Hecuba

" . . . and Zeus destroyed me not, but is still preserving my life,
that I may witness in my misery fresh sorrows surpassing all before."
~Euripedes, *Hecuba*

A woman keening might mean anything.
Other things than men and children
may be lost, run over by the big truck
of the gods, those eternally drunken drivers.
What has dropped from me has fallen silent.

I almost asked what I did to deserve this.
That old song. Let's say I wanted
not too much but too little.
Let's say my special hubris grew

inward like a navel. I have given birth
to nothing. I have tried to be a city.
And when the strangers sent their gift horse
my gates swung wide like legs.

Now it starts—feet first, then the creeping gray
cold up the shins. It's not that bad, really.
Next the crotch goes numb. There goes
the womb, that bag of old news.

So I am petrified. I might make a useful statue.
You can tell a tale by me. Oh, I edify.
In the wet slate cave of my chest,
the rattle of a small stone.

Petrified

There are a lot of ways to turn to stone
when living makes its true intentions clearer.
You can decide your suffering has seared you clean
as a tortured saint, nobody's got nothing on you
when it comes to loss, you've ascended to a zone
where pain hardens to shiny quartz, the best
expensive countertop that can't be burned.
You can arrive at truth as sharp and mean
as snakebite or a knife that cuts clean through
a ripe tomato. You can be you alone
deploying the diamond edge, the acid test,
a hissing canniness you've bloody earned.
Sister, Medusa waits in every mirror.
There are so many ways to turn to stone.

Peacocks at Andalusia

the O'Connor home in Milledgeville, Georgia

The former Mary O'Connor, there in her shapeless coat,
balanced on crutches, among the peacocks

at Andalusia. She knows it's not arthritis now, knows
it's lupus, the wolf that ate her father.

She follows the slow birds slowly, not so much
herding them as allowing them to lead.

One morning in a garden in California, might as well
have been Oz, I looked up from my coffee to see

a peacock wandering past, like flotsam from the night's
last dream. Revelation! Iridescent dispensation!

In my transport I failed to recall
last night's guest, biding her black time

in a web at the window, scarlet glyph on her back.
A fairy tale demands a witch.

In the calendar square for August 3rd, with 1964
pulsing in the distance, the obtuse Regina,

who never got the Godsmack she required, wrote *Death
came for Mary Flannery.* Like a gentleman caller.

On the silent film her daughter watches the absurd and useless
birds strut and peck, not waiting for him, only aware

he's on his way. Maybe he's something like them,
dragging his load of grandeur behind him in the red dust.

To the handsome foreigner who'd kissed her, she wrote,
I know they're stupid, but they have a lot to be proud of.

It felt, he said later, like kissing a skeleton.

Pre-MRI

There's always the chance it won't be nothing
so let's not fuck around. Let it be

big—softball, grapefruit. They never seem
to be ping-pong balls or cumquats anyway,

so make mine muskmelon or bread dough
swollen in the bowl. Regulation-sized

basketball, slightly deflated. Standard-issue planet,
maybe Neptune. Not Saturn, I don't need

those complications. Make it too big to bomb
or scoop, too big for anything but reverence.

Bring it, as I will bring my all to the plastic gondola
to lie and listen to the music of the spheres,

which turns out to be a Metal band.
Bring the sweet nurse with her needle,

her thorough explanations. Bring the affable
technician, conductor calling stops and starts.

Bring the photo of the skull beneath the skull,
memento mori swamping the whole situation

like a *guerilla jefe* standing in the *plaza*,
boots wide apart, announcing that the town

is his, resistance is futile. We will be
free now, he says, and he might be right.

He has a way with him. In one getup or another,
he's the one I've longed for since I was a swoony girl.

Now, swaying on the edge, I think why not
surrender, persistent as he's been, lurking

around my back doors with his black-eyed
greedy self. Bring him on. I'll wait in my dark

boudoir, my secret tunnel of noise, eyes open,
a song in my mouth—atonal, rude, all mine.

Still Life with Crows

She finally got what she imagined: a house
like a well-made sentence, everything

inherent, rooms breathing but deeply,
like Buddha—draw in the world

with its shrieking disasters and obscenities,
breathe out compassion's long slow note.

She got colors true as Easter eggs.
She got patina and texture and light, oh

light, she passed whole days watching the light
shift across the windows' shiny faces.

The silence hummed, uncracked
except by an occasional sound slipping

down from an upper room, a rusty croak.
Outside the door she'd stand and listen,

as bleat met caw across a furious flapping.
At times she seemed almost to comprehend

the discourse of guffaw and sneer, snark
and imprecation, raucous contradiction.

Beneath it all, a dark bass note,
vanishing when she tried to hear it.

Sometimes she felt a rising in her throat.
Sometimes she felt the weight of air

displaced by shiny, tar-black wings.

sternus vulgaris

the common starling

In the room that at the end of the house, dark,
where I flail for words, I seize on a shred of sound
outside, a scritching on the hardscape ground.
Framed by the window, a shadowy piece of work,
a motley vagrant. Gleams of purple-green
among the oily feathers, yellow beak.
Vulgaris. Mimic, bandit, squatter, sneak,
no tune worth the name to call his own.
He pokes around for lunch. And then, for no
reason on earth, it lifts, the shapeless thing
that's sat on me for days. Time, quivering,
opens a crack. He raises his head. The noon
gathers around his beak. He croaks his lone
bald note, what can only be called his song.

Perfect

Mostly I've known summers by nights
alone on the porch in the dark, cat in my lap,
night singers in full rasp and trill
after the birds have yielded the day.
Oceanic, those nights, so deep I could sink
to a reef of desire, a yearning surge—
endless, meaning it had no object. Pure
and fierce, the want at the core
of what's alive. This summer, the one
that left just days ago, brought a night
identical in every way but one—no reef,
no yearning. That might have been
the perfect summer night, nothing
to want, nothing left to want it.

This Edge

The coleus of June has gone viral,
strangling the impatiens I planted alongside.
Begonia begone, caladium collapsed.

Neighbors empty their pots and half-barrels,
mulching the remains. I let everything
degenerate in peace. One surviving

magenta bloom straggles alongside
flaccid stems, vacant soil. I like
this ambivalence. This edge.

The trees finally shake off the soupy
August sun. I study how they take
the thin, sharp blade of September light.

Their green begins to sour. Soon
the revelation, a better word
than *turning*. They do not turn,

the trees. What they do is let go,
release the green, baring the brilliant,
brief ferocity of what's left.

On His 79ᵗʰ Birthday My Brother Cleans Out His Garage

He finds a forgotten picture of himself with our father taken years before I was born. *You can see I'd been crying* he says. *So what do you think I did with it?* Maybe put it aside for me? *I threw it out!* he crows. *The bastard's finally out of my life!* He's waited all day for this, the drama's climax. It demands response. Well, congratulations, I mutter. *He's out of my life,* he repeats, and then, needing more from me, a coda, *and now he can be out of yours!* As if he's offering me the deal of a lifetime. I'm thinking: After six decades dead, it might be fair to say the bastard couldn't be much further out, or more securely in.

I'm the only visitor to the grave now. Last time I went, the flat rose-colored stone was harder to find. Mud-smeared, crowded with weeds and last year's leaves, it seemed to have shrunk. As I cleared it with Kleenex, the fishing lures swam into mind. Dotted and striped, trailing feathers, weird creatures from an undersea dream. Near them, sweet smoky ghosts curling in empty pipe bowls. Pipe cleaners at attention in their packet, waiting to be bent and unbent, spiraled around a finger, twisted into something else.

The day he died, three days before Christmas, I was pulled out of fourth grade at 2:00. My brother was waiting. He drove me home without saying anything except *I don't know* when I asked. Amazing that I didn't guess, given the endless hospitals. Amazing that he didn't tell. Both of us practicing some kind of innocence. He left the news to our mother to break. I cried then, almost like a girl who knew she'd lost something.

Spring and All

March cracked its swollen door just wide enough
for the old cat's skinny body to shoot through,
an arc of pent energy, wintered in for months.

An instant before I did, he saw twin chipmunks
jiving on the patio. One went left, for the woodpile,
the other straight for the rockwall.

Before a thought could cross my mind, the cat
was at the wall. At that point I might have saved
the littler life, even as it hung like a limp kitten

from my monster's mouth. I'd done as much before,
rescuing his prey. A cold gust rushed me. Everything
wavered on a cusp. I closed the door.

Maybe, I thought, the ferocious old imperative
should have its way. In that charged moment
where everything is hunger, maybe it should be fed.

I'm sorry, I said to the chipmunk, but what is
the cat's life, or any life, but hunger? When it comes
down to it, what is his life but your death?

A few days later, snow, wet and heavy,
bowing the daffodils. The cat forgot his hunger
for good. Forgot his ornate repertoire of yowls.

Forgot to move and then to breathe, and March,
slippery as ever, turned to April,
which has been described as cruel.

The Falling

March snow, sudden and thick in the library windows. Three carrels down, two students talking as if their lives depended on it. My mind does its sideways slide, like tires on new ice when a car seems suddenly weightless, and I think *let it all go flying, why not, let this life unravel like a long scar.* I watch myself spin away from the loves, the loyalties and meanings that have moored me, feeling the lurch in my stomach when my gondola went over the top of the double Ferris wheel at the state fairgrounds and for a moment before the ground rushed up I could see all the way to Canada.

In those days, when the snow was new and deep, we stood buffered in snowsuits, faces turned up, open-mouthed, catching flakes, and then we'd throw our arms wide, cruciform, falling back like timber or soldiers, buttermilk sky curling over us, inky trees, and then the soft *whoof* into snow. We lay there, breathing, face to face with the great blank winter sky. Then we flapped our arms and legs like stranded birds, planing arcs into the snow. But first there was the falling, the giving in to gravity, as if in that lush surrender we forsook ourselves, took wing.

Plague Spring

April, with its sketchy reputation,
slouches down the empty streets.

Spring slinks in, announced
only by birds, those that have survived

our company. Days pass
like a silent slideshow. Me, I seem

to have a gift for quarantine,
the product of long practice, like most gifts.

If you knew me in kindergarten, you knew
I'd secure my perimeter in yellow cardboard bricks.

If you knew me in high school, maybe
you knew I wasn't really there

in Joanie's car as we smoked and drove
past one guy's house or another's.

I was in lockdown, sure as girdles,
sure as curfews, sure as fantasies

kept dark and tight. It's second nature
now, honoring distance, avoiding touch.

Making do with what's available like
some pioneer woman. Being fine.

Outside my back door, something—
birdsong, a tuft of breeze—recalls

a dark blue cotton jacket, zippered, soft,
and a puddle quivering in a driveway.

There was once an April when
I stood in my blue jacket, sprung

from months of muffling, breathing
the forgiving air, studying water.

II

The End of Wildness

Eve, an Apologia

> "When the woman saw that the fruit of the tree was good for food and pleasing to the eye, and also desirable for gaining wisdom, she took some and ate it. She also gave some to her husband, who was with her, and he ate it." ~Genesis 3:6

They seemed like three good reasons—
life, beauty, wisdom. As I stood there,
breeze slipping between my legs, toes curling
in the new earth, nothing whispered in my ear
but a dragonfly. The rule kept making
no sense—that we who knew no good or evil
must avoid the evil of the tree. A hard lump
to swallow at two days old, when the tree
made its own case. That reach of my brown arm,
the pull and snap, the sweet bite, those were
the most innocent of motions.

As for the rest, there were no seductions
in that place. I saw the man and said,
"Have an apple?" Later, cornered, he hurled
the core to the ground at my feet.

The penalty was pain in childbirth,
or sorrow, depending on your translation.
I had enough of both to pay for an orchard.
My boys—you know that story. Meanwhile
the man became a wilderness, convinced
I was his damnation. And then my girls—
of course I bore girls, otherwise the book
becomes a pamphlet. On my unstoried daughters
the curse fell hardest, girls who begat
girls who begat hungry girls, all looking up
at fat red fruit, wanting to know.

Oval

Rabbit Egg

The book was large and thin, shiny dark green, and it had no words. A baby rabbit, small and brown, curled inside an egg, fast asleep. Outside, in the world, a duck studied the egg lovingly. The duck pecked and kicked at it, jumped on it, rolled it down a hill, but the shell held and the rabbit slept, curled into itself, bigger and bigger for every page. Finally the rabbit was full-grown, still cramped inside the now-huge egg, quiet, four feet pressing against the inside of the shell like a giant pushing against the pearly shell of a sky, having outgrown a perfect, fragile world. The egg cracked, finally, and rabbit woke to duck, to this weird love waiting as if it were meant to be.

Fractured Skull

If there were a film it would show Mary's head ricocheting back off the tree and hitting mine, the back ridge of her skull slamming into my broad, flat forehead. The big kids got blamed for letting us go down on the toboggan without one of them. How new we were, to have hung on as the tree rushed toward us, to have been too frightened, too rapt in speed simply to fall off, roll away into the snow. I had a big lump, navy blue and green. Mary had a fractured skull. She hadn't yet shed her cloudy baby tongue, so she said it was *fwack-shode*. She disappeared from kindergarten for long weeks, and we felt her absence like a small ghost. When she came back, wearing a soft pink-and-white wool hat, it was as if she were an angel returned from some edge we hadn't known about, where her head, now fuzzy bald like a new chick's, had cracked and some of her pale lisping life had seeped out.

Silly Putty

It came in a plastic egg that fit in your palm, split lengthwise. Inside, it lay protoplasmic, fetal pink. It didn't harden or pull apart like clay. When you bit into it, your eyetooth sank and then popped through, as through a rubber lip. We pulled it like taffy, rolled it into worms or into balls we bounced off the floor or desktop. We pressed it down onto newspaper and then peeled it away, drawing up the faces of Nancy and Sluggo, Snoopy, Archie and Veronica, a bold headline letter, a scrap of news. Then we'd stretch it, distorting the faces, elongating the story into parody. Finally we'd fold it into a mouth that chewed and swallowed letters and colors, working them back into the pink, graying it to beige. Putty took it all in, even the funnies we didn't understand, the news we wouldn't hear for years.

Memento Mori

Inside an alcove at the back of the shop, curtained off, the shelves are crowded with *calaveras*. Death dancing naked through life's occasions—milling around a table laden with food at a Christmas; comparing blonde and red wigs before a mirror; fronting a band in a red dress. Many skeletal weddings, as if marriage were the biggest joke of all. As if the death's head in the corner of medieval paintings, the *memento mori,* had taken over the whole picture and declared a fiesta.

Knee bone's connected to the thigh bone, we sang on the playground. My father was our *memento mori,* grim at the head of the table while we worked our way around him. By that time the flesh hung on his bones. They lowered the casket, big and shiny as a Buick, into the hard December earth on wide straps, under a steel-gray sky. *The worms play pinochle on your snout.* I was born when he was nearly fifty. The cold had set into the marriage and he hadn't expected another child. Maybe I passed for some kind of redemption. Children who lose parents become fatalists. We're the ones who are sure spring will be late, the pain is cancer, the lover will leave. A shadow lurks behind all attachments, a crow's wing cutting across a corner of sky. Death is the silent player at the table.

In a picture taken on Christmas morning sixty years ago, my father holds me in front of the fireplace. In the mirror above the mantel he takes in the whole room—his mother, his wife, his son; a tree shining with fragile German ornaments, gold tinsel, silver icicles; himself, and me in his arms. All but the dancers, the uninvited guests, jaws open in silent laughter, giving no reflection.

The End of Wildness

We didn't know we lived at the end of wildness.
We never saw the trees cleared so our fathers
could plant new ones, thin and tender, roots
balled in burlap, anchored by wires hooked
to the grassy sod rolled out in slabs by our fathers
after whatever grew before was torn away.
We found enough of wild to feed our animal hearts,
the empty lots with hip-high weeds and fat burrs
that grabbed our socks, brown belly-pods
full of white silk, possibly poisonous berries,
garter snakes, yellowjackets, daddy longlegs,
the hedge between our yard and the Webbs'
where we slipped inside the cool dark green
to be invisible and far away, the big old maple
holding down the yard, with thick, elbowed
limbs to climb above a trunk well of black water
stinking with rotting leaves from other summers.
We knew the mean dogs to avoid and we believed
in horses. It was later we learned that we stood
at the end of wildness, not just where it ended
but where it was ended. We'd been brought there,
we learned, to save us from wildness. We were there
to be domesticated, as we taught our Brittany spaniels
sit and *stay*. We were there to unlearn wildness,
drive it from our hearts and bodies, across
the vacant lot where the Courtneys would build,
out past the marsh on 14-Mile where our mother
saw the heron once before the temple went up,
out to Woodward, then down, down past
the country club with its misty, sculpted greens,
past the zoo, where it was locked up so we could pay

to look into its eyes, all the way down to the city,
where, they told us, it ran loose, snarling, hissing,
the city we were learning to forget.

Basement

This is my Father's world goes the hymn. Uncle This and Uncle That herd with him down here below the world of women and their talk. On the round felt-covered table sits a carousel. Tuck the stack of waxy blue Bicycle cards in the angled slot on top, crank it like a jack-in-the-box, watch the cards spit out neatly into six bays around the base. Next to the table, under the stairs, is a paneled bar. On the counter stands a little naked boy in silver metal. Stick him on a bottle and pee-colored Canadian Club streams from the end of the fat silver penis he holds thoughtfully in his hands. There are two doors down here. One leads to the furnace room. We huddle there next to the big pipes and vents on summer afternoons when the radio says a tornado is coming. The other door is locked. No one goes in without him. This is his workroom, where the power tools live. Just inside the door, attached to the thick lip of a high table, is the vise. Crank another handle and two dense iron bricks slowly move toward each other to hold things still so he can saw them up. Put your left hand inside and turn the handle with your right. As the big jaws come together, feel the cold metal, then a push, then the squeeze. One more crank, one more. Imagine your hand spreading like pie dough. Imagine your whole body flattening like clay under this pressure.

Manface

I learned where a table's head was
because he sat there. Presiding
is what he did. Goad and gripe.
I wished him away, up north
shooting deer, hooking trout,
or in the hospital, leaving the table
headless for the three of us.

When he presided, dinner got dense.
Silence thickened, mashing words
like junked cars into small cubes
heavy enough to flatten you.
Brother chased peas around a plate.
Mother looked like a headache
or an August storm about to break.

His head at the table turned us stony
but it was transparent, a ghost
furrowing the air. I saw through
to the wall behind him. In the quiet
of my head I said a name. *Manface.*
Daddykins Manface. Gray impostor.
Barenaked emperor. Old pretender.

I knew no pity for his pain. Sucking
misery from his pipe, he saw his death
coming like a V8 Ford. He'd lost
a wife, a son, some body parts. I suppose
he knew he'd never know me. Soon enough
I was free to eat dinner in peace.
To ferret out some kind of life.
To find him everywhere.

Facts of Life

Starlings

The birdhouse sits on top of its own pole in the back yard, three stories of holes and perches under a sloped roof. Big and white, it reminds me of the country club where we eat prime rib on occasional Sundays and swim in the summer. It is a house for purple martins, but starlings try to move in. "Oh, those *starlings!*" my mother hisses, running outside toward the birdhouse, flapping her arms. I wonder why it matters which of them gets the house, why one kind of bird is better than another. "Starlings are scavengers," she explains. "Common. They take over other birds' homes, they'll roost anyplace." Oh, I say, but I wonder who decided in the first place whose house was whose.

Slowly I learn to tell them apart: the martins, compact, scarce, not purple at all but velvety dark blue; and the starlings, long and loud, flat black flashing brown-green. I begin to see it, how one is better; why we want one and not the other. I need to understand these things. I begin to worry about the martins, urging them to be quick, to stake their claim. When my mother charges out after the starlings, I watch from the window, wondering who will win.

Burning

Our living room is full of grown-ups. I am small enough so that their talk seems to float up over my head, a buzzing cloud. I am outside the room, unseen. My mother is telling a story. Her voice is low. It seems to be about a fire, a big fire in a city, in Chicago, a long time ago. Someone's apartment was burned up. *And when they found her, she was sitting in a chair, burned so badly they thought she was a colored woman.* She whispers the last words.

The story follows me to my room, circling me like smoke. I think about fire coming into your house. I see the firemen coming in, walking around, turning a corner and seeing her sitting there. I knew that fire could hurt you or even kill you. But now I know something else. You can be burned so much people won't know you. You can change into someone else, a stranger.

In my imagination I keep creeping around the corner to look at her again. The room is undamaged, pristine, beige and rose, pale and quiet. All the fire has condensed in her. The woman sits motionless in a wing chair, blackened, smoking, waiting.

Waterfall
for Rhys

We walk through town to the park with the waterfall in the river, my girl cousin and I. It's wide but not high. You can climb stairs up the banks on either side and stand at the brink, watching the silky green water suddenly crumple and drop. Big kids dare each other to walk across on the low cement wall built to make the water tumble.

We get to the top and stand, panting, laughing. The spray cools our faces and wets our blouses. Then we see them, or we hear them. Maybe we just sense them—boys, a group of boys, older boys. We know when they see us. We try to be inconspicuous, absorbed in our own conversation, keeping our eyes away from them. But they head straight for us, like dogs on a scent. They surround us, loud and laughing. With one mind we scan our options and try nonchalance, aiming for a narrow space between dangerous bravado and a show of fear, knowing either one will provoke them like the sight of blood. "What should we do?" says one, prompting another to say, "Maybe we should throw them in!" All of them laughing.

We turn to each other then, my cousin and I, and our eyes lock. Into the air between us rushes a knowing we could never name, one we don't know we possess. We are making a choice that is already part of a repertoire we don't know we've collected. In perfect accord we both burst into tears. It is like a taut cord snaps. The boys guffaw and shamble off, leaving us at the lip of the waterfall, still held in each other's eyes until we can no longer hear them, only the rushing water.

Belle

It had to be a rose, for the story.
I'm not really a rose girl. But if I'm to be
a tight little bud ripe for the plucking,
it must be a rose I'm swapped for.
If a father steals a daisy or a zinnia
for his girl, that's just a distraction.
A lot of girls are daisies, some are zinnias,
but not those fed to beasts. Which is not
what I would have called him. I never
called him anything. I knew him
by his damp earth smell. I knew him
by his vast rough tongue. The wet
leather of his snout. The eyeshine
when he came to me at dusk. He took me
into him like a taste he'd forgotten
from the forest. I burrowed in him,
I shuddered and hummed. When
the thorns tore his hide, the flash
of gold lamé seared me like flame,
without surprising me. Again the story,
its requirements. Knowing an end
when I come to it, I traipsed home,
where no questions were asked
and nobody wanted to know.

Mother, North by West

"It's like they are two halves that have been separated for years."
~Joe Mantello, director of *Wicked*

1.

I'll give you this: you could make an entrance.
Charm, aplomb, *noblessse oblige.*
Who else could carry off that dress?

Your hand wanded over us all, shedding
tolerant fondness, comforting
the little people. I was never that small.

Among girls unfolding like flowers,
my pushy boobs strained the gingham.
So visible I was, easy target.

A flick of your fingers arranged things.
One disdainful laugh did for the wicked.
How could I ever own the scene like that?

Start walking, Miss Fancy Shoes.
Easy for you to say, rising like Jesus,
bubbling back into the pastel sky.

2.

People come and go so quickly here. Who knew
when you'd show up, all smoke and drama,
always *in medias rage,* trailing the black jetstream

of your history, hurling fireballs. Curses
on our presumptions, our little sagas!
How dare the small and meek complain

about their journeys? *Long? You call that long?!*
And there it was, my name across the sky like
a warrant. Why was the weather always

my story? To what could I surrender?
You'd loom up in my glass, sarcastic acid-green,
the bloody sands forever running out.

People come and go. Balloons get loose,
and dogs. Houses drop, buckets overturn.
As you dwindled to nothing,

I heard you in the hissing steam.
What a world, you croaked. I touched
your vanishing hand. What a world.

When Andrea Graddis Pierced Her Ears

When Andrea Graddis pierced her ears
the whole school knew by noon.

Some of us wondered if she'd finally gone too far.
No one American had pierced ears.

It was hard to know what Andrea thought,
sailing down the hall, meeting no eyes,

books riding her slightly swaying hip,
two girls flanking her and two more trailing,

already wondering how to get their mothers
to let them do it. The boys catcalled

while their eyes slunk after her, blinking
at the small flashes of gold just above

where her hair, which might have been frosted,
curved forward to her jawbone. This was after

John Glenn but before the president
got shot and everything began to happen.

Years later, that October Saturday night
when I was alone in the dorm and couldn't think

what to do about myself and drove a charred needle
through my ice-numbed lobes, bloodying

the bathroom and launching twin infections,
I thought of Andrea, wondering what it took

to be the first girl in the known world to pierce
your ears, whether her eyes ever came to look

sideways or back, where she learned
to walk like that, in the face of everything

coming at us in the opposite direction.

Transcript

Art History

In the dark room you blink at the *Bedroom at Arles*, throbbing blue and gold on the screen. The professor speaks of tragic irony—this warm, cheerful picture emerging from the last days of his final summer. He painted it three times; clearly he found peace at the end. The other students seem to agree. You turn back to the screen—quavering bed, bucking floor, dizzy window, walls veering at odd angles—and try to see. You think maybe you're as crazy as he was.

On Saturdays you take the El downtown to study the paintings face to face. Past the great stone lions, up the staircase, to the right, into Nineteenth Century Europe. Eventually you know the works spatially, by where they hung. On slide-identification exams you think *left of the door in the big gallery* and *across from Cinco de Mayo* and *next to Duchess Pigface*. Before leaving you check the *Bedroom* to see if anything has changed. The room *must express unswerving rest*, he wrote to Theo, *the compulsory rest recommended for me*. In this, the second version, flat light from an invisible source fills the room. The walls are a lurid chalk-blue, the now-particolored floorboards disintegrating, sliding. The casement windows trump the eye, folding in, now folding out. Framed pictures lean out sharply from the wall over the bed. You feel the guard's eyes in your back as you move in close, trying to see.

By the time the train surfaces north of the Loop, the early November dark is settling down over the city. The tracks swerve sharply up against the backs of apartment buildings in abrupt, startling intimacy. Fire escapes, second-floor back doors, lighted windows framing a table, a bed, a brief human figure in silhouette, there for a moment, then past. *Lives*, you think. *All these lives going on*. You stare through the blurry train window, image after image escaping behind you into the night.

History of England I

That May, when the National Guard shot the kids, *Music from Big Pink* was playing. The frozen waves had finally melted back into the lake. We were on strike, wearing red arm bands, rejecting Business As Usual. There were rallies and speeches every day. I wandered through it all and pondered what I owed to history. Especially English History, the class I couldn't bear to boycott. The professor, a very famous guy with three names, slipped us a hint about the final exam: it would require, he said, *a knowledge of dynastic succession.* On my way back to the dorm, past the barricade on Sheridan Road, I realized the only safety lay in memorizing the English monarchs, Conquest through Glorious Revolution, all the Henrys and Edwards, the occasional Mary, one blazing Elizabeth. As May turned to June, while the battle against Nixon went on two blocks away, I spent the hot, sweet nights on my bed with the chart I'd made, eyes closed, repeating over and over, like a meditation chant, *william first, william second, henry first, stephen, henry second, richard first,* fathers giving way to sons who became fathers seeking sons who would usurp them, on and on toward a three-hour exam where I would write their names in order, flawlessly.

Geology

You had to take one science, and rocks seemed reliable, knowable. But instead we seemed to study waves a lot. The motion of waves, which had always seemed up-and-back, in-and-out, turned out to be circular. That undermotion you couldn't see, where the fallen wave drew down and back, dragging the shore along under the new wave rising. A circle, but complicated, troubled. I studied the diagrams on the board down in front in the huge amphitheater and heard the waves outside, behind the building, hurling themselves over the jagged rock breakwater, clawing at the campus, biting away the lakefill. It was the first time I really understood that water makes sand, that pebbles and stones are half-digested rocks on the way to sand.

I thought of the scissors-paper-rock game. I could never remember what beat what, which was more powerful. Why would paper cover rock? Paper wouldn't have a chance against rock. Finally I saw it made a circle: rock bent scissors, scissors cut paper, so paper had to have something over rock. Something always giving way to something else.

I'm not sure we ever got to rocks. I remember only waves, surging, curling, falling, sucking back. I understood them later, in the melancholy-long-withdrawing-roar Matthew Arnold heard out his honeymoon window. *Fun guy,* I thought, *wedding night and all he can think about is beach erosion.* I thought of them when I lay under one of the Geology T. A.'s on a bed full of coats in an apartment down in Rogers Park, too drunk to get home, while he pushed and urged and then, when I pushed back, drew away, *I'm sorry, I'm sorry,* the room spinning. I felt the waves at the edge of my life there always, on and on, *water covers rock,* like some theorem I could never decipher, *water covers rock.*

In the Office in the Afternoon Following a Class
in Women's Literature

She is pregnant—do you see that,
boy chemist sitting beside my desk?
You have never felt as small as in that chair,
lost and dumb in poetry. Yes, in line two
something kicks her in the ribs. But no,
it's not her lover this time. It is the thing
inside her, upside down, and that's why
in line one she exclaims about connection.
I wonder—when you catch a ride
home to the suburbs on the weekends,
do you ever think about the woman
who opens her arms to you and your laundry,
your tales of the dorm, the girlfriend,
the bastard chem prof? The woman
who nods smiles, murmurs, thinking to herself,
He is so serious, absorbed in his things,
manlike; does he sleep with her?—do you know
she carried you around for three long seasons,
leaping in her heart when you first moved?
Do you know that once—thumb in mouth,
curled into yourself almost as you are now
in that chair, likewise waiting to be delivered—
you dealt her such a shot to the ribs
that she gasped with the sudden woman's sense
of all she would learn of love and pain,
how one curls like a fist inside the other?

Triptych

Heart Rendering

After twenty years of their papers, certain mistakes grow predictable, like *conscious* for *conscience*. What can you do about kids who confuse awareness with guilt? So I feel it coming: this student, moved by the novel, will call it *heart-rendering*. My hand moves to circle it, then stops, as if the ligaments were yanked tight. *Render,* from the Frenc *rendre,* to give back, to give up. Render unto Caesar, render unto God. *Render,* in English, also means to translate or alter. After burying two husbands, my mother married a man retired from the rendering business, who had buried a wife. For twenty years he winnowed down the carcasses of animals until the fat ran thick. Even though I know they do this with chemicals, I imagine ungodly heat, great steaming vats, the fat that insulated cows and horses melting into something else, some rich and humble, an extract useful for soap or candles. I think of the hearts going last, big fists of muscle finally giving up, releasing. I stay my corrective hand. She's right. We live through our unrelenting years, we give ourselves up. We know the heat and are translated, clarified. We are heart-rendered.

Mary Alice
  for Kate

Thinking all week about justice, I was ambushed by a pure sadness. I was driving into the first spring evening that promised summer, letting my mind go violet and soft, and there you were, May Alice, striding along, tall and rawboned, brown hair pulled back in a rubber band, jaw like an axeblade, eyes knit up with pain. Someone doesn't love you back, or in the same way, or something. You don't tell me more, and why should you, why should I need more, who doesn't know this story? As we sit in silence, white blossoms raining down on the car, I realize there's nothing to be said to you. Sometimes we are not loved back. The primal injustice. Violation, outrage. Our hearts deserve their desire. And yet there is no fighting it, no Take Back the Heart march. I can give you nothing but my passenger seat, a hand on your shoulder, some breathing room in the last moments of a day. You don't want your prof's esteem tonight, you want the love you were born for. I would give you justice if I could, Mary Alice: I would give you one who hears you, as I do in class, and thinks, *God, what a beautiful, swift mind.* I would give you one who watches you run across the campus, long and steady, and thinks, *She runs like a deer, what a heart.* One who glances into your naked face and says, *Those eyes—she is incapable of lying.* I would give you a world where girls like you stand under trees on evenings in late May, white blossoms snowing down, knowing it's all for them.

Matryoshka

At the end of their first college term, they are in mourning for themselves. One says it hurts to know she'll never be that girl again. Another says it scares her to know the girl she thought she left behind came with her, dragging the whole city of Saginaw behind her. What's worse, I wonder, loss or repetition, that everything changes or that nothing does? I tell them, for what it's worth, that I think of us as matryoshka dolls: our former selves nest inside us, younger selves inside them, in almost limitless regression. Some days I can barely feel them in this tenured menopausal body. Some days they're live and crowding like puppies, needy and ridiculous. But if life twisted me apart at the middle, there they'd be: thirty-eight, limber, striding up to forty, thinking maybe there's room yet for a kid, wondering if she will always be alone; inside her, twenty-eight, girl in woman's clothing, doing her bad Italian lover in her office between classes; inside her, eighteen–eighteen, like them—desperate to know and be known and certified smart; inside her, eight, a little sister, a girl with an imagination as well as a father who helps her onto a blue bike. And inside her—a darkness, a silence. Screw them all back together, chest to hips. Tuck them all away inside each other, keep them safe. Something of each of them comes to class for me to know. Sometimes I see us all—the students, the teacher—in retrospect, a future memory, dim and shredded. I wonder what we will remember of each other. One or two, if they recall me at all, might think of the matryoshkas.

Four or Five Witches

1.

I was absent. That seems to be the crux of the matter. Do not underestimate what it means to be the Uninvited. Not once, but time and again. It marks you, this watching the world's play from the bushes outside the window. Studying the girl at the center of it all, the dawn-colored girl, laughing like crystal. Such watching makes you ugly and fearful. At first you cower and hide from children, little brutes who say out loud what their parents swallow, but over time children begin to run from you. You steep in exclusion, aging, darkening, while she stays always the same, like a recurring dream through a hundred-year sleep. Dogs bark at you, backing into their withers, neck hair standing. Young men off to catch hummingbirds for her entertainment throw rotten things at you as they pass.

Then you start to see that without you, she has no story. This magic of yours is hers turned inside out, as if you were her shadow. The power to make roses wither and men slither away on the ground. The power to bring the party to a screeching halt. To freeze her father, gaping, spit in his beard; her mother, sheep-eyed and gasping through her corset; her prince rusted shut in a showy bow. Then you can get a good look at her, up close. Let's scratch the seashell flesh, see what's inside that smells like lilacs and tastes like honey while you stink and bleed like any beast in the forest. Somebody prick her, see if she's real. Somebody wake her up.

2.

Red, something red. One day the blood comes down again, after two dry years. Comes like torrents of unborn children, in near-black clots and carmine shreds, and with it the red hunger. Specific and insistent, won't let me rest. I walk the room all night, afraid. In the mirror, I'm green with it. *Not fair, not fair,* I whisper, and my face goes watery and then, slowly, becomes hers. With her ruby lips and her ruby shoes and her red, red heart. Her father's gift from god. Little mother in a land of little men. The wind begins in my womb, circling and widening up and out, dark and pointed, lifting me from the ground. *Send the woodsman with his shiny blade after her heart, feed it to her little dog. Turn her loose in the dungeon where the royal lions pace. Crucify her in a far field where she can hang till Christmas, scaring the grackles.*

When I wake, the blood has stopped, perhaps for good. I go to the mirror again and study. Far back in my left eye, something deep red on a silver dish, moving toward me. *I have eaten my own heart,* I think. But then I see an apple, held out to me by an unseen hand.

3.

Hair's the first thing to go. First dry, then thin, then dim, as if the light in you has gone out. Whatever curl it had gives up. I laugh, remembering the spells of youth, the chants for waterfall hair, thick and shining, its own sleek animal. This is the magic all the young girls beg me for—hair that will hide them, speak for them, protect them, warm them. Hair to replace the fur they've forgotten. Hair a boy can climb by night. And me with nothing to give them but a moonstone and white sage to burn.

So wouldn't you know I'd get the girl with the epic hair? Hair so consuming it left her exhausted. *You want magic?* I said. *Cut it off!* But she only stared at me, with my ragged efficient graying mop. I slapped the pity from her little heart-shaped face. *At least I can walk across the room without falling over backward! Is he worth it?* And you know, her dense little eyes said he was, that and more. I could feel it when I came back and he'd been there, smell him in that hair. One night when he was one hair short of too late, I saw it in his eyes, spikes of light in them, like thorns. *You want power?* I said to her. *Cut it off!* But she only looked at me, with eyes that said she knew all about power. And so that night as she slept, that ponderous head on her arms, I took it. Hank by hank, I took it.

4.

Your children are in the woods. I didn't bring them here. They wandered away from you, bored or curious or full of themselves. I am trying to make the most of this, and it isn't easy. I build candy houses for them while *I* survive like my sister the crow on the crumbs they drop along the way. I leave signs for them, stick figures and scrawls on trees, the smell of sugar and little songs on the wind. I make them cover the same ground over and over until they get it right. I bend the river back to meet them. The boys fatten on their own importance, the girls starve and apologize. I prod them with sticks as they sleep, trying to stir the right questions. I encourage their mythmaking, their moviemaking, their mapmaking. I would do the same for my own, if I had any. Which I don't. They are horrible, really. So hungry. They'd have eaten me out of house and home. So I came to the woods, knowing sooner or later they all come here, thinking the trees belong to them, it's another Wilderness Experience. I let them get good and scared. I make sure they smell death in the rotting leaves and logs. I want them humble, shaken. But they are never lost. I find them.

III

Toward Water

Year of the Horse, 4688

"As the traveler who has lost his way throws his reins over the horse's neck and trusts in the instincts of the animal to find his road, so must we do with the divine animal that carries us through this world."
~Ralph Waldo Emerson

Under lowering cover of January, it's easy
to swear by sleep, to accept resignations.

Can you believe in something else?
Something moving toward you, not slowly,

something running? Just before sunset,
light breaks from the west.

The clouds thin to a blue mane
streaming over the withered hills.

In the dark, wind whinnies in the eaves,
waking you from something

huge, strong and real between your thighs.
Blood beats down the canyons

of your ears. Listen to the heart's gallop:
something comes unbidden,

unbridled, ungentled, the gift horse
you never asked for, the horse

of an unnamed color, the color
of rivers, of an infant's iris.

This is your one sure thing. It comes
in thunder and it comes for you,

a single question in its obsidian eyes:
Will you trust it enough to let go

the reins, to let it carry you
where you're going?

Conversation

Between two glasses of beer lies
a silence that might stretch
as far as we could pull it.

It is something we do not talk about,
a silence swathed in silence, something
you might sense when I fail

to laugh, nod, frown, question. Then
you hear it, something like the sea
far off at night. For you, an inkling.

For me, a tidal wave, this silence
beneath the roar and sob of history,
born of loquacious men and artful women

who soothed and smoothed and took their thoughts
to bed. Between a man and a woman,
there is always something unspeakable.

Night, the Berkshires

Daylight drops away and scenery
reverts to wilderness. The mountains hunker
like beasts, long spines stretching
out against the black sky. Wild things
run alongside us at a distance.
Far up in the hills, a lone light
races past and vanishes. How many times
have we been down this road?
I shiver and reach to turn up
the heater. Speeding around
a long curve, you smile at me
and reach to change the station.

Star-Crossed

Along the interstate, southbound,
the commuter crowd thins, leaving me
alone with the sudden stars,

which now begin to move.
One rushes toward me, blinking,
seeking a place to light.

Another veers sharply, shooting
out across the sky. Some flash me
urgent coded messages,

others constellate to tell me
stories in which I figure as the hero.

The night is shifting, realigning.
The queen rises from her chair to hail
the startled hunter, who drops his studded belt.

The water bearer stumbles, splashing
the virgin, who gasps and opens her eyes.
The archer looses a shaft at last,

nicking the shell of the crab, who goes
sidling off toward morning.

Navigating By Hand

1.

A witch took one of your hands,
noting how it was at once
pristine and paw-like, perfect cuticles
above patches of dark fur.

She turned it over, scanned
your palm's cartography, and told you
it didn't work: this head line
slicing across like an Interstate
built to get from one place
to another with minimal fuss
or scenery—but then this heart line
cutting a ragged ravine through the flesh
like some rutted country road
unknown to maps but memorized
by fishermen in search of the secret
turn of the stream where trout
swim shallow in the sun.

This is a map to nowhere, she said,
bound to get you lost.
You unfolded your handy smile
and told her it worked perfectly:
the one carries all the traffic,
the other no one needs
to know about.

2.

When, in the bar as we watched the band,
I reached without moving my eyes
across the uncharted air between us,
hooked the curl of your finger, the small one,
with my own, then eased myself
gingerly into the palm's soft belly,
I was finding my way blind,
fingertips moving like wary feet
through the underbrush toward that narrow
trail winding down to where I hear
water diving over rocks, almost see
fish leaping up to light.

Mud Season

Even the mountains withhold themselves.
They hedge their purple bets. Flood likely
as frost these days, cold sun as leaden wind.
Wheels sink into the hills they try to grab.
Deep ruts freeze, thaw, freeze again
into iron ridges. We get nowhere.

It seems so old, this earth, this struggle
to inhabit the places where we wind up,
to move through what holds us,
sucks us back. Our lives lie between us
at night, obscure and rigid. At dawn
we barely remember our dreams.
I watch the inscrutable hills
for what might propel us into April.

Cold Front

"Worlds are altered rather than destroyed." ~Democritus

Overnight an arctic breath
froze the river. But near the banks

at the thin dark edges of ice,
the water still sings, quietly.

When I come upon these dead
zones I find I keep on,

until these too become known
features of love's surreal

and lawless waters. Then I see
there is no end to love

or to rivers or to any of it.

Seney Stretch

"... that mind-numbingly monotonous 30 miles of M-28 between Seney and Shingleton that's the most direct route from the Mackinac Bridge to Pictured Rocks and Marquette." ~*Hunt's U[pper] P[eninsula] Guide*

The rush of the Bridge long gone, the shoreline raveled away behind us hours ago. We're in the Seney Stretch, bald, unforgiving slash of concrete, straight as a look from God. Only scrub pine between us and the Great Nada. Nothing to do but set the cruise control and settle in. The afternoon drops down like anesthesia. What is it we once said to each other? Easy to believe, by mile 15 that we've driven right out of our lives. Motion so unswerving it amounts to stasis, terrain so unredeemed it makes you want to weep. Easy for the mind to stagger off into the gnarly little trees reaching from the swamp, never to be heard from again. What kind of faith could reel it back in, like a brown trout? What is required to cast your lot with language again, or love? For now, for the duration, it's enough to fight off sleep. Keep the mind's eye open. Conjure the big lake coming closer, the ancient pictures in the striated rocks. Imagine cruising down into a town, toward a place where we have reservations, where they will know our names.

Marquette, Tuesday, September 11, 2001

While you interview for the job
I walk around Presque Isle beside
the quiet, dark-blue lake.

You'd already left when I woke
to the towers sinking into themselves.
A blank space has opened in the world.

Fall already singes the fingers
of maples arching the path.
Soon the lake will grow ferocious.

The bright sky is closed for business.
The country grounded. ATMs down.
I consider our ready cash.

I try to imagine a life here.
Would it feel like the edge of the world,
winter closing over half the year?

Later, with you, the day will get real.
Tonight, a rental on an inland lake.
Steaks on a grill, corn in a pot, cold beer.

A phone to call our people.
Beginning the return to our life,
the world ending somewhere else.

The Bride Wore Black

which should have been the first clue.
She ambled down the south aisle in her new, cheap shoes
while the groom came down the north in the dark blue suit
men buy one of, for weddings, power meetings, funerals.
Dinah Washington sang *It's very clear, our love is here to stay*—
Jesus, in a Greek play that kind of hubris would get you
castration or blinding or a raptor at the liver. Instead
everyone had omelets, made to order by a deft and silent man
behind a table in the great old mansion on the hill overlooking
the last day of the year. A blizzard was on its way across the plains,
and nobody would get out. Meanwhile everyone smiled
and made their choices, spinach, gruyere, scallions, mushrooms.
Mimosas blossomed from the open bar. She flapped and stumbled
through it all: What was she doing here? Who said her life
had anything to do with strawberries tipped in chocolate,
ornate seating charts, Polish crystal etched with names and date?
Who was she kidding, moving around the room,
dazed and footsore in those shoes, failing to see his eyes,
him in the dark suit, waiting for her to be done with this,
the man standing quiet as a cyclone's eye, slowly disappearing?

Just Night, Just Dark

The first question from the buzzcut
boys in the brown uniforms:
Were you two arguing or something?

They were too big for the room,
as cops always are, even young ones.
No, I said, I didn't run him out,

this is not that scene. It's just absence
we have here, sheer and bottomless.
Just night, just dark. Just gone.

Next time we spoke, after the dogs,
voices, lights, frogmen in the river,
the EMTs laboring over him,

when the boys in brown reappeared,
it was I asking the question, they
who corrected me. *He's gone* I said

isn't he. And then there was a pause
while they gathered themselves
in their protocol, standing there

after midnight in a funky old cabin,
young guys in the middle
of a woman's collapsing life.

Finally one of them recalled the words
and said *He is deceased.*

"Write a poem in the voice of a widow whose husband has drowned."

a prompt by Maura Stanton

What does a widow's voice sound like?
A low wind?
A lowing manatee?
A lowly inmate laughing like a loon?
The hinges of a door everyone keeps forgetting to oil?
A bird of prey?
Something drowning?

Invent any story you like.

If you wind up with one you don't like, write another.
Use your imagination, that's what we're here for.
Did her husband perish in pursuit of a great fish?
Does the fish really have to be white?
Was he trying to swim the English Channel?
Trying to save a child who had not waited a full hour after lunch?
Is he a hero? A fool? A victim? Is she?
Maybe it turns out he didn't drown at all:
Did he fake it and run off with a green-eyed bartender?
This widow, let's give her a backstory.
Was she a real ballbuster? Did she marry him
for money? Power? Security?
Do you imagine these are different?
How long was she married to this drowned man?
Would you believe four months? No?
What would you believe?
Does she discover his body, washed up
on her shore? Or maybe a piece of his clothing,

a shoe. One shoe toeing the waterline. No.
Nobody will believe that. Knowing
how much is too much—such an important
part of the craft.

This is an exercise in empathy.

Can you get inside the head of this woman?
She might be from another planet, where husbands
are specters and water is deadly and the years gape
like mouths and something is always screaming.
Do you care about the widow?
Do you care about the husband?
Do you care about the fish, the kid, the bartender, the English Channel?
Do you care about the water?
How deeply do you care? Deep enough to drown?

How does the widow feel about this particular river or lake or ocean?

First, make up your mind: is it river, lake, or ocean?
What is its name, in what Indigenous language?
Does she refuse to look at it?
Does she want to drain it dry?
Does she see it as her enemy?
Does she see it as an angry god?
Does it tempt her? Does she want
to marry it, marry it, marry it?
How do you feel about water?
Does it ever scare you?
Does it ever tempt you?
How well can you swim?
Can you imagine drowning?
Can you imagine a husband?

Can you imagine a widow?
Can you imagine?
Can you?

Pentecost

"And suddenly a sound came from heaven like the rush of a mighty wind, and it filled all the house where they were sitting. And there appeared unto them tongues as of fire, distributed and resting on each one of them. And they were all filled with the Holy Ghost and began to speak in other tongues." ~Acts 2: 2-4

Christmas Eve in a church unused to magic,
mystified by darkness and candles, little tongues
wavering in wine-red glasses in our hands.

You stood talking to the other mothers,
one arm draped in angel costumes,
the other ringed in tinsel haloes.

Looking for the miracle itself, I raised the glass
to see the watery flame. I never felt it leap
to my head, only a small hiss, then the smell.

I made no noise. I felt no burn.
Without a sound you turned
and smothered me in angel robes.

Around me, voices. Still I didn't speak.
I knew I would be blamed, though
the fire had jumped to meet me.

The Spirit left me then in my stink.
When it lit on me next I was alone. You were
years gone, and there were no angels.

Mother, the big wind blows and blows.
Beneath my crown of flame, I wait
to feel my throat erupt, to speak in tongues.

Toward Water

In mind I go to that stretch of Coster Road out past the county line,
where its shoulders drop off into swamp, the dead
trees stretching their wracked arms up from the water—
the land of hopeless trailers walled in plastic sheeting,
ducks and chickens running in yards, a plaster Virgin or small
American flag circled in painted stones. At every other driveway
an *Exit Realty* sign or some threatening scripture—
not much on mercy, mostly hard choices, immutable fate.
Posted, the trees at intervals declare, *No Trespassing.*
Folks have their half-acre of the north and not much else.
When I picture that part of the road, I usually move on
past the alpha and omega, day care and nursing home,
where we joked we'd wind up, on to where the road narrows,
dropping down to the river, over Rainbow Jim's little bridge,
the tunnel of pines, and then the driveway curling back
past the weeping fig we planted, hunched and thin
like a starveling refugee landed in the wrong country.

But today I remembered driving the other way, toward town,
that day you spotted the turtle making its way from water to water.
How you swerved, passed it, slowed, pulled over. How you got out,
walked back, lifted it, carried it across, put it down on the bank.
As we drove off, I wondered what it's like, a god's hands
seizing you, speeding you across the asphalt faster than
you've ever moved, setting you lightly down at the very edge
of your obscure turtle desire. Is it terror you know then,
flying over the ground, or does a nothingness come down
like a shell, stilling you until your webbed feet touch earth
once more and life starts to move again, toward water?

The turtle slid into the rest of its life, as we did. That day
we were out for a three-store grocery haul, a good lunch, check out
the whitecaps on the bay and home by dark, beyond which you
were headed for the river, the mindless river that gulped you down.
It seemed to me I stopped then, but I was only moving
in another layer of time, so slow it felt like stillness.
I was creeping across a long, straight road, a roaring
bearing down on me, no hands to lift me, carry me over.

I came back to the life I was assigned

and locked the door behind me. It was still,
breathing as I'd left it. I moved smoothly,
as I used to enter water. I knew where
to find my needs so long as they were kept
in check like dogs well schooled but leashed.

Is this, at last, what constitutes damnation,
to sleep in your own bed and rise to a day
entirely your own, to know each room
by heart, and how the sun comes in, and why
the bird-shaped letter opener, broken-tailed,
lies on the desk just there? To be sent home,
summarily returned to the old order,
where nothing is designed to save you?

Jackson

"Chase, 72, and Zigler lived together for 10 years. In December 2010 though, Zigler died in his sleep at age 67. Instead of letting go of her good friend though, Chase ended up keeping him in the chair in which he died." *~Jackson (MI) Citizen-Patriot*

Sometime after you've made it beyond the worst of the worst, you arrive in Jackson. Jackson is halfway between Here and There, but for you this is it. Jackson is where you live now. Park, walk around. It looks a little stunned, this town, a little shaky. The streets are a mite too wide for the traffic. Downtown is five blocks of buildings that have all been through too many incarnations to matter. At one end is the Carnegie Library, elegant and composed, like a dowager whose money used to run the place. At the other end is a kind of plaza at the feet of a tall, shiny structure topped with a corporate logo. It looms over the lesser buildings like the motivational speaker who strides into a windowless conference room at the local Best Western in his blue suit and brilliant smile, eager to tell the sparse crowd how their lives could change. A shrine, this building, but the new god blew town one night. Nobody believed in it anyway, or if they did, they're getting over it. Everyone's getting over it here. Don't think the place has given up, though. Jackson doesn't give up. Jackson has acquiesced, which is different. Jackson goes on.

Downtown gives way quickly to gray and brown houses on small lots, a beauty parlor called Magic Touch, the Quality Market. In a small white house on Cooper Street a woman watches NASCAR with her boyfriend, who died two years ago. "I didn't want to be alone," she says. "He was the only guy who was ever nice to me." He could always make her laugh. She keeps him clean, she says, he doesn't smell. They've lived together ten years. "It's just that after so many bad things happen to you, I don't know."

Further out at the west edge of town lies the little municipal airport. On a rainy evening, drive along its chainlinked perimeter, out beyond the runway. In the fog the lights are vague. Nothing is flying tonight.

Devastated

It's what everybody says they are now.
Your favorite restaurant goes out of business,
you're devastated. Your kid doesn't make
the swim team—devastated. Your one-nighter
fails to call again—you get my drift.
No one hears in the word the cities burning
or sees the ruined fields. It means *laid waste,*
as in *Getting and spending, we lay waste
our powers.* Wordsworth, what's he on about,
I ask my students. Nobody has a clue.
They think he means we throw our powers away
like waste, like Styrofoam, or that we waste them
(whatever they might be, these powers
of ours) like money—not entirely wrong, yet
not right. OK, try Jagger then: *I'll lay
your soul to waste?* Nope, nada. Within
the hour two or three of them will say
they're devastated by their grade or some
abrasive text appearing on their screen.
Words—what can we say about them? Slick,
absorbent, malleable, they mostly fall
apart. And then again, sometimes they hold:
two strange Englishmen, poised at the dawn
and dusk of the industrial West, imagine
the soul as ravaged, leveled landscape, void
of life or color, or of movement, save
the smoke meandering from exhausted fires.
I don't know how to tell you my story,
but if I say that for a certain while

I was devastated, I want you
to smell the fetid smoke, to see the dog,
starving and cankerous, nosing the waste.

IV

Parable of the Mountain Lion

Man Held in Burning of Homeless Woman in Los Angeles

"Mr. Petillo threw a flammable liquid on the 67-year-old woman and then set her on fire on Thursday. Local residents said she was known as Violet and eked out a living by recycling cans." ~*New York Times*

The first thing Adam did was piss, a long arc
into the forest. Since God had given him the power
of naming, he called it conceptual art and found it
very, very good. He would have said
the sunlight made it look like gold,
except that of course he'd never seen gold.
Instead, he said it made him feel free. Later,
it made him a full professor. Still later,
a bit longer after the earth had grown cold,
Mr. Petillo threw a flammable liquid on the 67-year-old.

Free also grows cold. Free gets lonely. There must be
something to love and loathe, something for the heart
to beat against. On Sunday let us make
woman. Make her kind of vague but all too clear.
On Monday we'll dissect her so we can solve
the mystery we made. We'll unmake her, make her stay
unmade. On Tuesday woman will make us
a house, we'll occupy her, she'll be settled.
On Wednesday we'll bedeck, betroth, betray
woman, and then set her on fire on Thursday.

Wednesday's woeful child was Daisy, a name
her mother planted, imagining another girl.
Saturday's child, who must work for a living,
had only her own good name, which was Rose.

Much good did it do her. Monday's Lily, fair of face,
slipped hard on a gentleman's piquant triolet.
Friday's child, loving and giving, was Iris.
She crumpled fast for lack of light. But Thursday's girl
had farther to go, with a baggage cart for a cabriolet.
Local residents said she was known as Violet.

This is it, the baggage left uncollected, wherever it is
we've all arrived. Anyway, we're here. L.A. got cold
that week; the rest of the planet seems to be rolling
backwards, toward flammable. Meanwhile, the good
park bench. We'll wake soon enough when the match gets thrown.
Heartless and homeless, the destiny that is man's
(which I use in the generic sense, of course). The alien
scientists a millennium hence will call us conundrums:
This was a people who pissed where they ate. They made no plans
and eked out a living by recycling cans.

". . . a court in Cardiff, Wales, once again released Thelma Dennis, 50, to get therapy for her addiction of making bogus emergency telephone calls, even though she has been prosecuted about 60 times in 24 years on similar charges. In an earlier case, Dennis agreed to a therapy that sent painful shocks through her body every time she dialed 999, and she remained free of problems for four years but reoffended recently by making up a bomb threat against a store." ~*Northern (MI) Express*

Number Nine? Number Nine? Number Nine?

There is a bomb. There is a gun. There is a burglary. There's been a kidnapping, an abduction. There's a note. There's footprints all around the house. There's a broken window. There's a dog barking. There's been a forced entry. There has been a violation.

Nine. Nine! Nine?

See, nine is the limit. Nine is the end. After nine comes nothing, you're back to zero, see? You have to go back to zero. Nine is as far as you can go in this world.

Nine is three times three. Three times nine is nine nine nine. Don't look upside down or you'll be done for.

There's a face at the window. There's a car without headlights. There's a sick dog. There's someone crying next door. There's a wild animal. There's screaming from the chemist's shop. There's shouting from the schoolyard. There's something in the sky. There's someone in the TV.

Nine ladies dancing. Nine to five. Engine engine number nine.

There is electricity all through my body. There is fever all through my body. There is remembering all through my body and forgetting all through my body and there is offending all through my body. I have offended. The best defense is a good offense. I have reoffended.

I try to count to ten first. I don't make it quite.

There is a man who looks suspicious. There is a man who looks like an Arab. There is a man who looks like my dead father. There is a man who looks like the prime minister. There is a man who looks like he's on drugs. There is a man who looks like Jesus. There is a man who looks like he wants something. There is a man who looks like Charlton Heston.

Ninety-nine bottles of beer on the wall, and her shoes were number nine. The whole nine yards.

One step after nine ninety nine and you've gone too far. All you get is a one, see, plus all those zeros. You try it. You try it on your own car.

Nine is a comma. Also an apostrophe. Nine means something else is coming. Nine is a tadpole, a sperm. Nine means something else. 99 problems. Nine has a secret.

Someone has been hurt. Someone's gone missing. Someone misses something. Something is missing. Someone has been hurt.

Number Nine? Number Nine? Number Nine?

Do You Memorize Me?

found in my inbox, in its entirety

I want to suppose that this letter goes
to the right person and you memorize me. Hi!
I had no possibility to message you earlier
by reason of some occasions at work.

Though several weeks have passed.

But I have sent this letter in the hope
of your reply. Do you memorize me?
I am Nastya. If you forgot my age I am 33.
When we communicated last time, I mentioned

I seek a deserving person for something serious.

I am not interested in discussing sex. I have no desire
to exchange fantasies or nude photos.
I don't want a person who is married or who seeks
simple entertainment.

I seek only a deserving person.

I let you know it initially to eliminate
any misunderstanding. That's why if you seek
the same as me, I will be contented
to get your answer and I want to learn you more.

In spite of spidery of COVID 19 and there are a lot of stints.

Who knows, when it is over we could meet

and view interesting places. I have been dreaming
to go to Banff National Park and Upper Canada Village.
Probably you could accompany to view these places.

War Stories

A father's love is dangerous.
What son wouldn't die for it?
What red-blooded boy wouldn't mount
the slab and stretch out
while the old man hones the blade
glinting in the moonlight,
both whispering *See, Father, see
how I love you?*

And when the righteous hand is stayed and the blade
falls to the earth, they both rise up,
feeling blessed, lucky, grateful for their lives,
which they'll rededicate, they'll sacrifice,
they'll make a religion of this.

No end to what a son will take
in the father's name —
thorns in the skull, nails in the hand.
He'll drink vinegar and swear it's wine.

He'll hang crosswise in the wind
for hours believing he'll wind up
in his father's arms.

Night comes on. Saturn rises
in his monstrous hunger.
He raises his sons in his clumsy fist,
tears them with his dogged teeth.
Their blood slides down his chin,
he crushes their bones to pulp,

sucks down their hearts and livers and
loves them, oh, man, oh, brother,
how he loves them.

The Auschwitz Photographer

> "I didn't return to my profession, because those Jewish kids, and the naked Jewish girls, constantly flashed before my eyes. Even more so because I knew that later, after taking their pictures, they would just go to the gas." ~Wilhelm Brasse, AP interview

The child is shot from three angles. Right profile, so you see how aggressively the head was shaved, the tufts and bald patches. Face front, wide white forehead, dark eyes almost stern. And finally the head turned right, eyes lifted toward the ceiling, pointed chin, and now a plaid scarf tied almost rakishly around the head, as if it were a costumed portrait. A boy, a girl, hard to tell shorn, body lost inside the too-large wide-striped prison suit. Number two six nine four seven.

"I must have taken forty or fifty thousand," he recalls, nearing 90. When he landed there at 22, his past as a photographer's assistant saved him. Not Jewish, just a Pole who tried to flee. You can see in his fleshy, sad face the gentle boy he was. Modest, well brought up. So when the beautiful doctor in his impeccable uniform brought the girls, mostly 15 or 16 but some his own age or older, what could he do as they removed their clothes, faced front, ineffectual hands fluttering, turned sideways, turned around, shoulder blades and hip bones pointing, breasts shrinking? "I tried to address them politely," he says, and maybe they felt that as they turned and turned and turned.

He remembers one man by name, Zylinski, from Gdansk. A red and blue tattoo covered his back, Eve handing Adam the apple, the tree arching over them, the coiling serpent. "Gorgeous," he remembers, "really beautiful." A work of art. He saw it three times: once when the man removed his shirt and turned his back for the photo; again through the camera's eye, which he could not help adjusting carefully to capture all the detail. And then, maybe a month later, a friend who worked the crematorium said he had something interesting. A large square of skin, tanned. The tree, the naked woman making her offering to the naked man.

"I saw it," says the photographer.

Just ahead of the Soviets they evacuated him to Austria, where the Americans found him, weighing 88 pounds. He returned to Poland, but never took up another camera. In his dreams they crowd against the dark gray backdrop, the girls, hungry, huddling in their innocent skin.

In School

"Things that I witnessed and experienced in that place—if the words
came out of my mouth, I think that would be the end of me."
~Garry Gottfriedson, Indigenous poet and survivor

Transformative is among our favorite words,
we who believe in school.

It is hard work, changing a child
into something else,
but it can be done.

First, remove the tongue.
Bury it in an obscure location.
Everything else will follow.

Look—he is still afraid to speak,
all these decades later.
He thinks he will disappear,

as if words were magic.
And they are, they are
transformative.

A new tongue is a kind
of salvation, a rebirth,
as we know, we

who have always
believed in school.

Parable of the Mountain Lion

"In Blairsden, a caller reported that she could hear a woman screaming.
A deputy said that it was probably a mountain lion."
~Portola (CA) Reporter

In Manitou Springs, a paperboy reported that he saw a mountain lion on a
rock.
The ranger said it was probably a dog.

In Portland, a bank clerk said her last customer looked just like a bull
terrier.
The branch manager said she would probably get fired.

In Okemos, an old woman reported a fire.
The station chief said she was probably crazy.

In Springfield, a girl said she thought she was crazy.
Her mother said it was probably the weather.

In Elmhurst, the minister said God had sent the devastating weather.
The kid in the back row said He was probably drunk.

In Erie, the 7-11 clerk said he saw a truck run over a drunk.
The manager asked if it could have been a Humvee.

In Waycross, the biology teacher said she'd seen a Humvee full of soldiers.
The swim coach said they were probably skinheads.

In Dover, a mailman said there was a houseful of skinheads two streets
over.
His customer said they were probably terrorists.

In Davenport, the lawyer said she'd flown home sitting next to a terrorist.
Her husband said he was probably CIA.

In Salinas, a woman said she thought her husband might be CIA.
Her sister said maybe he was psychotic.

In Tempe, an English major said her boyfriend was psychotic.
Her roommate said men are dogs.

In Kingsley, a motel clerk said something had torn up his dog.
The night manager said maybe it was a mountain lion.

In Provo, a ranger said he'd heard a mountain lion the night before.
His wife said it was probably a woman screaming.

Lupercale

"Italian archaeologists last month unveiled an underground grotto that they believe ancient Romans revered as the place where a wolf nursed Rome's legendary founder Romulus and his twin brother Remus. A few feet from the grotto, or 'Lupercale,' the Emperor Constantine built the Basilica of St. Anastasia, where some believe Christmas was first celebrated on December 25 . . . to coincide with the Roman festival celebrating the birth of the sun god..." ~Kalamazoo Gazette

He's seen the new light, our emperor has.
And by this light he does his winnowing
and transplanting. It simplifies, this light.
It clarifies and orders. Its radiance
searches out our chaos, the brawl and surge
we make our way in, we children of wolves.

It's said that all roads lead here. That's some kind
of order, it would seem, but if you arrive
to find a thousand random, randy gods
translated from the Greek, seized from Egypt,
purloined from Abyssinia or Persia,
all occupied in ancient gripes and grudges,
all raving for somebody's wife or daughter,
or wine or beeves or other tasty bits
to feed their pride, what order have you got?
Or so our emperor sees it, I'm quite sure.

Myself, I'll miss our messy pantheon.
Exasperating, yes—I'll grant you that,
but at the least, one never lacked for stories

when nights got long or children couldn't sleep.
One story only, says the emperor,

is real. And so our hungry little mouths

are plucked from pointed, pendant lupine dugs
and fastened to a smooth and blue-veined marble
virgin breast, and we're good as new.

No further tribute to the fierce, the furry,
the yellow-eyed and snaggle-toothed. Instead
a quiet winter rite to sanctify
the sun's birth, which is now miraculous.

The light returns to us this time each year.
The sun keeps faith, whatever name we choose
to give it, more reliable than gods
or emperors. This day, as I was walking
out in the western hills beyond the city,
I watched it slip away. Along a ridge,
stark black against the dying orange light,
a long-limbed shadow paced.

Solstice Eve

for Diane

It is the whitest restaurant in America.
Even the one Black man is fading.

The booths are packed with doughy Midwestern
women in Christmas tree and snowflake sweaters.

They order the soup-and-sandwich special
or the chicken fajita roll-up and Diet Coke.

As the waitress comes by to ask if everything's ok,
the snow starts. It will go on all afternoon.

The woman whose one child is driving five hours
home today chews and worries about the roads.

The woman with a black hole eating through her heart
smiles at her friend's jokes. The one who's wakened

heavy with dread every day for weeks talks about
the Fraser fir she got half-price. Another spoons

chowder to her lips while something
in her head shrieks *love me, dammit!*

The snow will fall, thick and quiet, all night.
Tomorrow is the shortest day of the year, and then

the longest night. Once, thinking it would swallow us,
we howled and stamped around a fire, chanting back

the sun, begging not to be left in this darkness.

2020 Vision

It took opening night and opening day. Took opening.
Took teachers from kids from streets. Your job, your plan.
Took your best friend. Took your first and last breath of spring.
It took your bar, your movies. Your mom. Your man.

We're in it together, it said, then took together. Took you down
and pressed your life out, shot you as you ran and in your bed.
Split your spine right through your kids' eyes. Stalked into town
with a nasty tattoo and an AR-15 , locked and loaded.

It spun the Gulf. Seared the West. Took trees old as gods.
Took medics, millennials, mailboxes, voting booths,
and then took Chadwick B and RBG. Switched out the odds
on logic or love. Worked over the sorry truth

and sold it cheap. Taught your preacher not to pray.
The bastard blew your mind. It took your breath away.

Rainbow

"They can't explain why rainbow trout have appeared in Spirit
Lake." ~News report on Mt. St. Helen's, 10 years after

1.

They have theories. One posits a poetic underground river — *caverns
measureless to man*. Another holds that some tough specimen, some
evolutionary militant survived against all odds beneath the mud,
gills barely flaring, pulling in trace wetness until the years had done
their work.

Either way there's magic of a sort, or miracle if you will. That lake
was pronounced dead; we all saw the pictures: a hissing bowl of
sludge in a grayed-out landscape, color doused like flames. Now in
the slowly clearing water, a quick tail, a flash, bands of pink, green,
silver.

2.

He likewise saw its promise, the captain of that floating zoo.
Standing on deck with a giraffe or two, he watched that band of
color arc above the flood like a truce flag or the track of some great
hand waving away the past. Then he understood. After the keel
plowed into Ararat's flank and things had dried out a bit, he joined
the talk of forgiveness and new covenants, but when he sat by
himself at evening, watching the water's slow retreat down the
mountainside, he felt it all around him, the benign, if not divine,
forgetfulness infused in all things. Even now the count of couples
hopping, slinking, creeping up the gangplank slipped away from
him like the water down the slope. Soon, he knew, he would forget

the press of them, the warm stink, the bleats and growls of fear and hunger and annoyance, textures and shades of fur and feathers, scale and horn. *And they have forgotten already,* he mused, *the terrible rocking, the sickness and stench, predator and prey indifferent in their intimacy. Now,* he thought, watching a she-wolf trot along a ridge with five shambling pups, *they remember nothing but their own natures and hungers.*

His tired eyes turned back to the water, where just then the sunlight broke on a flashing arc of silver-pink. *The ones I couldn't save.* He laughed. *But what salvation could they use? Why should they care if it's fire next time, the fish, with nothing to forget or to remember? The fish, who cannot close their eyes.*

Acknowledgments

I'm grateful to the editors of these publications, where particular pieces originally appeared, sometimes in slightly or significantly different versions.

The Bridge: "Mud Season," "Night, the Berkshires"

Calyx: "In the Office in the Afternoon Following a Class in Women's Literature," "War Stories"

Contemporary Michigan Poetry: Poems from the Third Coast, Ed. Michael Delp, Jack Driscoll, and Conrad Hilberry (Wayne State University, 1987): "Eve,

An Apologia" (as "Eve")

A Face to Meet the Faces: An Anthology of Contemporary Persona Poetry, ed. Stacey Lynn Brown and Oliver de la Paz (University of Akron, 2012): "Hecuba"

Folio: "Man Held in Burning of Homeless Woman in Los Angeles"

Fourth Genre: "The Auschwitz Photographer," "The Falling," "Oval"

Great Lakes Review: "Jackson" (as "Nothing is Flying Tonight")

Hotel Amerika: "999"

Juxtaprose: "Pentacost," "Pre-MRI," "Still Life with Crows"

Kalliope: "Solstice Eve"

Measure: "Lupercale"

The Michigan Poet: "*sternus vulgaris*"

New Delta Review, "Navigating By Hand"

Passages North: "Heart Rendering," "Mary Alice," "Matryoshka," "Year of the Horse, 4688"

The Peralta Press: "Facts of Life"

Phantom Drift: "Four or Five Witches"

Prime Number: "English History I"

The Prose Poem: "4" (from "Four or Five Witches")

Quarter After Eight: "Basement," "Geology," "Memento Mori"

Room: "2020 Vision"

The Southern Review: "Devastated"

Third Coast: "Rainbow"

Unsplendid: "Parable of the Mountain Lion"

Four of the poems in this collection appeared in my memoir *Grief's Country: A Memoir in Pieces* (Wayne State University, 2020): "Devastated," "The Bride Wore Black," "Toward Water," and "Write a poem in the voice of a woman whose husband has drowned." <u>Note</u>: The prompt from Maura Stanton that forms the title of the latter poem appears in *The Practice of Poetry*, ed. Robin Behn and Chase Twitchell (New York: Harper's, 1992). The italicized lines in the poem come directly from the text of the prompt.

Gratitude

. . . to Kelli Russell Agodon and Annette Spaulding-Convy for embracing this book and honoring it with the Wilder Prize. One of many reasons I'm proud to have the Two Sylvias imprimatur on my book is that you have centered the work of older women with this series. To Annette, thanks for grace in dealing with an epigraph-prone poet. To Kelli, thanks for superlative sleuth-work in finding both photographer and font in order get the cover I dreamed of, and particular thanks for applauding the opening line. I needed that.

. . . to Fran Dwight, for casting her penetrating eye on me and making it painless.

. . . to Bill Betts, for graciously allowing us to use his remarkable photograph of Omena Bay.

. . . to the Sunday poetry group: Kit Almy, Marion Starling Boyer, Christine Horton, Gail Martin, Nancy Nott, Susan Blackwell Ramsey, and, in memoriam, Danna Ephland, who invited me in. Having thought of myself as a prose writer for decades, I've been a hesitant poet. You are the context in which I finally determined to put a collection together, and I don't think it would exist without you. Special thanks to Gail Martin for establishing the helpful precedent of Gails from Kalamazoo winning the Wilder Prize.

... and most of all, to two extraordinary poets: Conrad Hilberry, who made poetry an open door and ushered me right in; and Diane Seuss, who has shown me, for over forty years, that trusting the imagination can be a way of life.

Born in Detroit, Gail Griffin grew up in the 'burbs and fell into a lifelong romance with the woods and waters of northern Michigan during the summers. After college and grad school, she returned to Michigan to begin a 36-year career at Kalamazoo College, teaching literature, writing, and women's studies. She won both college awards for teaching and for creative work/scholarship, and in 1995 she was named Michigan Professor of the Year. In the larger community Gail became involved in anti-racist work, offering workshops on the nature and implications of whiteness. She also leads occasional community workshops in memoir writing.

Through her work and relationships at the college Gail discovered creative nonfiction, which became her professional focus, and poetry, which has taken second place until recently. She is the author of four books of nonfiction, including *"The Events of October": Murder-Suicide on a Small Campus* (2010) and *Grief's Country: A Memoir in Piece*s (2020). Her essays, flash nonfiction, and poems have won Pushcart nominations, "Notable" designations in *Best American Essays,* and genre awards in journals. As her first poetry chapbook, *Virginals,* was appearing in 2021, Gail was sifting through 30 years of poems and found *Omena Bay Testament,* her first full-length collection. Though it looks mystical on the cover, Omena Bay is real. It curves into the Leelanau Peninsula, Michigan's "little finger."

Publications by Two Sylvias Press:

The Daily Poet: Day-By-Day Prompts For Your Writing Practice
by Kelli Russell Agodon and Martha Silano (Print and eBook)

The Daily Poet Companion Journal (Print)

Everything is Writable: 240 Poetry Prompts from Two Sylvias Press
by Kelli Russell Agodon and Annette Spaulding-Convy (Print)

Demystifying the Manuscript: Essays and Interviews on Creating a Book of Poems
edited by Susan Rich and Kelli Russell Agodon (Print)

Fire On Her Tongue: An Anthology of Contemporary Women's Poetry
edited by Kelli Russell Agodon and Annette Spaulding-Convy (Print and eBook)

The Poet Tarot and Guidebook: A Deck Of Creative Exploration (Print)

The Inspired Poet: Writing Exercises to Spark New Work
by Susan Landgraf (Print)

Omena Bay Testament, Winner of the 2021 Two Sylvias Press Wilder Prize
by Gail Griffin

At Night My Body Waits. Winner of the 2021 Two Sylvias Press Chapbook Prize
by Saúl Hernández

Nightmares & Miracles, Winner of the 2020 Two Sylvias Press Wilder Prize
by Michelle Bitting (Print)

Hallucinating a Homestead, Winner of the 2020 Two Sylvias Press
Chapbook Prize by Meg E. Griffitts (Print)

Shade of Blue Trees, Finalist 2019 Two Sylvias Press Wilder Prize
by Kelly Cressio-Moeller (Print)

Disappearing Queen, Winner of the 2019 Two Sylvias Press Wilder Prize
by Gail Martin (Print)

Deathbed Sext, Winner of the 2019 Two Sylvias Press Chapbook Prize
by Christopher Salerno (Print)

Crown of Wild, Winner of the 2018 Two Sylvias Press Wilder Prize
by Erica Bodwell (Print)

American Zero, Winner of the 2018 Two Sylvias Press Chapbook Prize
by Stella Wong (Print and eBook)

All Transparent Things Need Thundershirts, Winner of the 2017 Two Sylvias Press
Wilder Prize by Dana Roeser (Print and eBook)

Where The Horse Takes Wing: The Uncollected Poems of Madeline DeFrees
edited by Anne McDuffie (Print and eBook)

In The House Of My Father, Winner of the 2017 Two Sylvias Press Chapbook Prize
by Hiwot Adilow (Print and eBook)

Box, Winner of the 2017 Two Sylvias Press Poetry Prize
by Sue D. Burton (Print and eBook)

Tsigan: The Gypsy Poem (New Edition)
by Cecilia Woloch (Print and eBook)

PR For Poets
by Jeannine Hall Gailey (Print and eBook)

Appalachians Run Amok, Winner of the 2016 Two Sylvias Press Wilder Prize
by Adrian Blevins (Print and eBook)

Pass It On! by Gloria J. McEwen Burgess (Print)

Killing Marias
by Claudia Castro Luna (Print and eBook)

The Ego and the Empiricist, Finalist 2016 Two Sylvias Press Chapbook Prize
by Derek Mong (Print and eBook)

The Authenticity Experiment
by Kate Carroll de Gutes (Print and eBook)

Mytheria, Finalist 2015 Two Sylvias Press Wilder Prize
by Molly Tenenbaum (Print and eBook)

Arab in Newsland , Winner of the 2016 Two Sylvias Press Chapbook Prize
by Lena Khalaf Tuffaha (Print and eBook)

The Blue Black Wet of Wood, Winner of the 2015 Two Sylvias Press Wilder Prize
by Carmen R. Gillespie (Print and eBook)

Fire Girl: Essays on India, America, and the In-Between
by Sayantani Dasgupta (Print and eBook)

Blood Song
by Michael Schmeltzer (Print and eBook)

Community Chest
by Natalie Serber (Print)

Naming The No-Name Woman,
Winner of the 2015 Two Sylvias Press Chapbook Prize by Jasmine An (Print and eBook)

Phantom Son: A Mother's Story of Surrender
by Sharon Estill Taylor (Print and eBook)

What The Truth Tastes Like
by Martha Silano (Print and eBook)

landscape/heartbreak
by Michelle Peñaloza (Print and eBook)

Earth, Winner of the 2014 Two Sylvias Press Chapbook Prize
by Cecilia Woloch (Print and eBook)

The Cardiologist's Daughter
by Natasha Kochicheril Moni (Print and eBook)

She Returns to the Floating World
by Jeannine Hall Gailey (Print and eBook)

Hourglass Museum
by Kelli Russell Agodon (eBook)

Cloud Pharmacy
by Susan Rich (eBook)

Dear Alzheimer's: A Caregiver's Diary & Poems
by Esther Altshul Helfgott (eBook)

Listening to Mozart: Poems of Alzheimer's
by Esther Altshul Helfgott (eBook)

The Wilder Series Poetry Book Prize

The Wilder Series Book Prize is an annual contest hosted by Two Sylvias Press. It is open to women over 50 years of age (established or emerging poets) and includes a $1000 prize, publication by Two Sylvias Press, 20 copies of the winning book, and a vintage, art nouveau pendant. Women submitting manuscripts may be poets with one or more previously published chapbooks/books or poets without any prior chapbook/book publications. The judges for the prize are Two Sylvias Press cofounders and coeditors, Kelli Russell Agodon and Annette Spaulding-Convy.

The Wilder Series Book Prize Winners and Finalists

2021:
Gail Griffin, *Omena Bay Testament* (Winner)

2020:
Michelle Bitting, *Nightmares & Miracles* (Winner)

2019:
Gail Martin, *Disappearing Queen* (Winner)
Kelly Cressio-Moeller, *Shade of Blue Trees* (Finalist)

2018:
Erica Bodwell, *Crown of Wild* (Winner)

2017:
Dana Roeser, *All Transparent Things Need Thundershirts* (Winner)

2016:
Adrian Blevins, *Appalachians Run Amok* (Winner)

2015:
Carmen R. Gillespie, *The Blue Black Wet of Wood* (Winner)
Molly Tenenbaum, *Mytheria* (Finalist)

Made in the USA
Columbia, SC
15 July 2023